SHARKS

SHARKS

LEE SERVER

TED SMART

The Image Bank® is a registered trademark of
The Image Bank, Inc.

Printed and Bound in Spain

ISBN 0-941267-05-9

Written by: Lee Server

Producer: Robert Tod
Managing Editor: Elizabeth Loonan
Designer and Art Director: Mark Weinberg
Editor: Terri L. Hardin
Production Coordinator: Ann-Louise Lipman
Picture Researcher: Edward Douglas
Associate Art Director: Dana Shimizu Lee
Copy Editor: Irene S. Korn

For rights information about the photographs in
this book please contact:

The Image Bank
111 Fifth Avenue, New York, NY 10003

Table of Contents

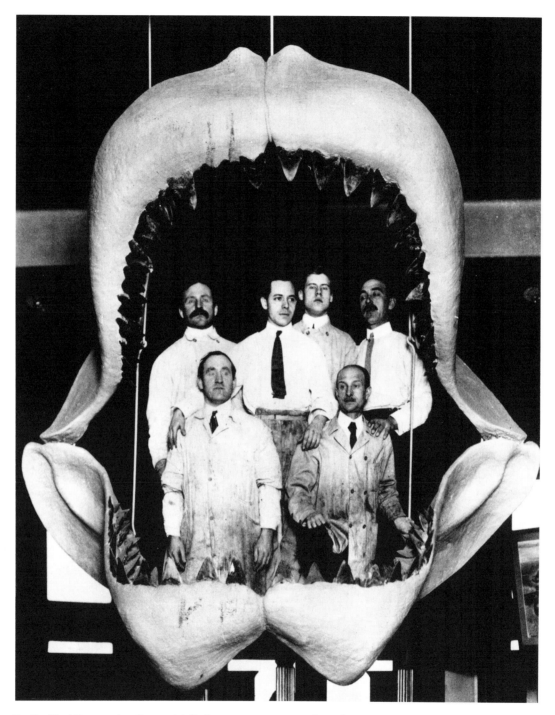

Dr. Bashford Dean and staff pose with his famous reconstruction of jaws from a *Carcharodon megalodon*. While these jaws are still on display at the American Museum of Natural History, a new reconstruction presently at the Smithsonian Institute has scaled down the size to approximately two-thirds of Dr. Dean's estimation.

INTRODUCTION

SHARK.

It is a word that has come to be synonymous with the powerful emotions it so often evokes: anxiety, fear, terror. For thousands of years, mankind has lived in frightened awe of the great predator of the sea. Whether fueled by the myths and superstitions of the past or the lurid depictions on modern movie and television screens, the image of the shark in the public's mind has remained constant through the centuries. It is an image of overpowering size and strength, savage ferocity and evil. As far as most people are concerned, the shark is a beast to be avoided or killed—nothing in between.

This narrow, phobic reaction to the shark is unfortunate. Many nights' sleep have been lost worrying about a fish whose man-eating appetite has been much exaggerated. But, more importantly, the conception of the shark as a "mindless killing machine" has kept the public from understanding the diversity, beauty and intelligence of the shark and has led to the slaughter of countless innocent and harmless species. *Carcharodon carcharias*, or the great white shark, with its hydrodynamic body and mighty jaws, is indeed a ferocious carnivore that will attack large animals for its prey, but it is only one of hundreds of different types of shark. Those different types include the ray-shaped angel shark of the genus *Squatina*, living along the ocean floor on a diet of crustaceans; and *Rhiniodon typus*, or the whale shark, a gentle giant which dines almost exclusively on tiny marine organisms. The majority of sharks are small, averaging little more than three feet in length, and most will tend to shy away from something as large and unusual as a human in the water.

Legend has had it that the shark's biology was primitive, that its eyesight was poor, and that it relied exclusively on the fundamental senses of smell and hearing to find its prey. Man's condescension to the shark has been proven misplaced. Not only are its ordinary senses complex and highly adapted, but it possesses something far more advanced than man's own sensory equipment—electroreceptors which can read the electric signals given off by objects in the water. The biology of the shark may, in fact, include other unusual and "advanced" aspects which science has simply not yet discovered. For one thing should be made clear: the scientific investigation of sharks is still in its infancy. New aspects—new species, even, are discovered each year. Marine explorers and researchers must reluctantly add question marks to much of their data.

From a 19th-century German text.

The Story of the Shark

Sharks have existed for an estimated 450 million years. They swam the earth's seas before and all through the rise and fall of the dinosaurs, and hundreds of millions of years before man first trod on dry land. Despite the extinction of species and evolutionary developments since the earliest known fossil records, the design of the shark is relatively unchanged. Of all the creatures from prehistory, the shark is surely among the few still thriving in the late 20th century.

Remains of the oldest known sharks are mostly fossil teeth and "denticles"—the shark's version of scales. The best preserved species is the *Cladoselache*, a veteran of the Paleozoic Era some 400 million years ago. The *Cladoselache* has been found in several Southern states in America, in rocks that were once the muddy floor of an ocean covering North America at that time. The sediments in this area allowed for quick, undisturbed burial of the *Cladoselache*, leaving us with some excellent fossils for study. Scientists have found amazing detail in these specimens, including one whole fish on which a certain *Cladoselache* had dined before death, still contained within its skeleton.

The *Cladoselache* grew to only about four feet in length. It had narrow jaws, a very limited supply of teeth (unlike most modern sharks) and a caudal (or tail) fin built for speed. The *Cladoselache* had no anal fin, and copulation was performed in some way other than with the claspers which compose the reproductive organ of the modern male shark. The *Cladoselache* became extinct around 250 million years ago, and many questions will remain unanswered about this and other early sharks of the Paleozoic Age—which included a diverse selection of shark species. In fact, previously

unknown species from this era are still being uncovered in America and Europe.

Sharks evolved very slowly. In the Carboniferous Age (between 350 and 250 million years ago), there were two main shark groups, the freshwater xenacanths, and the ocean-going hybodonts. These sharks were the contemporaries of the dinosaurs and died with them, to be replaced in evolutionary turn by the direct antecedents of the modern shark, with better swimming capabilities, sturdier spinal columns, and larger jaws.

The development of the modern predatory sharks seems tied in with the appearance of large, aquatic mammals—porpoises, seals, sea lions, whales—after the last of the dinosaurs. It is in this period—approximately 60 million years ago—that we find the remains of some of the first makos and great whites, the man-eaters of today.

The Miocene period (25 to 10 million years ago) was the age of the giant predatory shark. Swimming the seas of that time was the massive *Carcharodon megalodon*. These sharks grew to at least 40 feet in length and some scientists have doubled that estimate. The existing teeth of this monster are the size of a man's hand.

Modern man knows little enough about the underwater world, so it is not surprising that early encounters the ancestors of man had with the creatures of the sea were obscured by ignorance, superstition and exaggeration. Sailors spread tales of monstrous creatures that could swallow up an entire ship in their massive jaws, stories probably sparked by the frightened sighting of a 40-foot whale shark or basking shark. When shipwrecked seamen were attacked and eaten by predatory sharks, illustrations of the attackers were highly speculative, depicting nightmarish gargoyles sent straight from Hell. The scholar Herodotus wrote, in 492 B.C., of the huge sea "monsters" that plagued waters off the coast of Greece. Even in the time of Columbus, the shark was not named or accurately described. In the 16th century, an English ship's captain named John Hawkins caught a large pelagic ("ocean-going") shark, probably a great white, and put it on public exhibit in London. Although the specimen did not have the serpent's tongue and rhino-like horns of the more fanciful illustrations, the real thing was sufficiently startling to cause a sensation among Londoners and provoke a faddish interest in sharks, not unlike the *Jaws*-mania of the 1970s.

It was in this period that the word "shark" entered the English vocabulary. The derivation is not known for sure, but likely comes from a German word, *schurke*—meaning villain. Such an appellation indicates that from early on, man's shark-consciousness concerned not the numerous gentle, harmless species but the relatively few ferocious predators. The shark became a totem of evil to millions of people who had never seen one—nor had even seen an ocean for that matter. William Shakespeare considered the shark a sufficiently devilish creature to include it in the ingredients of his witches' brew in *Macbeth* (Act IV, Scene I):

Scale of dragon; tooth of wolf;
Witches' mummy; maw and gulf
Of the ravin'd salt-sea shark;
Root of hemlock digg'd i' th' dark....

Scientific investigations of the full range of shark biology and behavior were far in the future; the bulk of the first recorded eyewitness accounts of man meeting shark, from the 16th and 17th centuries, were blood-soaked. A seafarer's report, from 1595, is typical:

This fish doth great mischiefe and devoureth many men that fish for pearls. As our ship lay in the River of Cochin, a Sayler being made fast with a corde to the ship, hung down with half his body into the water to place the same upon the hookes, and there came one of those Hayens, and bit one of his legs, to the middle of his thigh, cleane off at a bit, and as the poor man was putting down his arms to feel his wound, the same Fish at the second time did bite off his hand and arme above the elbow and a peece of his buttocke.

It would be hundreds of years before anyone would seriously try to determine *why* sharks attacked men. Of course, in all those years, few people besides shipwrecked sailors and overboard fishermen would ever see a live shark face to face. If the shark was a creature of danger and evil, he was a distant one.

But then, at the end of the last century, swimming and going to the beach became, for the first time, a popular pastime in America, Europe and elsewhere. Inevitably, some of these splashing bathers became victims of shark attacks. In the 1900s, a great white killed four people at a New Jersey beach, sending shockwaves along the whole North American coastline. And during World War II, fighting at sea and in the air put many wounded sailors and fliers into shark-infested waters. It was tragic that many men who had just barely survived one battle lost the next against sharks frenzied by the survivors' commotion and the presence of blood in the water. Hundreds of deaths were attributed to sharks. The U.S. command faced a crisis, with servicemen's morale undermined by fear of shark attack. The U.S. Office of Strategic Services instituted a research team to find out how to deal with the problem. They quickly learned that very little knowledge was available—not merely what objects in the water attracted or repelled them, but their number of species, their habitats, diets or even how they gave birth. Scientists had to face the fact that a creature found in every sea in every area of the world was a complete mystery to them.

Sparked by a combination of fear, wartime strategy and scientific curiosity, the first real shark research began. The discoveries in the years ahead would often surprise and amaze and—at times—serve only to deepen the mystery.

The Shark in Close-up

Until recent times, it had been a long-held belief that all sharks had the same narrow set of characteristics. It was believed that because of their being relatively unchanged from the earliest times, sharks were primitive creatures; mindless and aggressive brutes.

In fact, sharks are quite varied in size and shape, with some species, like the angel shark or the hammerhead, evidencing extreme modifications of what we tend to think of as the "classic type" shark. Furthermore, sharks have brains and body systems of some sophistication: they are capable of much retention of knowledge, and their behavior is the result of complex interaction between hearing, sight, smell and electrosenses.

It was, as well, falsely believed that all sharks were lone predators, cruising the seas in solitude except for short mating sessions. Actually, while some species like the great white spend most or all their lives alone, a number of other species (again, the genus *Sphyrna* or hammerhead, is an example) will travel in schools, or groups, of their own kind.

Like a number of other fishes, sharks practice social segregation by size (smaller sharks steering clear of larger ones); but they also have been known to practice sexual segregation. In some species, such as *Prionace glauca*, or the blue shark, male sharks may spend the summer in warmer waters while all females will go to the chillier waters in the north. And what of the belief that the large predatory species—the requiem (or whaler) sharks—were constant swimmers? Part of the shark's demonic image was this popular notion that it was cursed to swim the seas forever, its entire life, never stopping, never sleeping. We now know that these sharks may gather in dormitory-like caves where influxes of fresh water occur, and they will tranquilly rest or sleep, sometimes piled atop each other as if in bunk beds.

Obviously, the concept of the shark as no more than a brainless killer is woefully out of date. The shark is a most complicated creature and many of its capabilities are only just becoming understood by science.

There are approximately 350 different species of shark. Although sharks represent just one percent of all species of fish, that percentage may be increasing while you read this. Many new species have been found in recent years, including one exceptional find: the discovery of *Megachasma pelagios* or, more popularly, the megamouth shark. Indeed, less than 20 years ago, the total number of species was thought to be only 250.

Sharks differ from the majority of fish in that their skeleton is not made of bone but of cartilage. (Cartilaginous fish include only sharks, rays, skates and chimaeras.) Cartilage is the rubbery, collagen-based material we find in our own bodies in the nose and ears. It is a more flexible material than bone—which it becomes with the addition of calcium phosphate deposits. In the water, the shark's cartilaginous skeleton makes for the graceful and sinuous swimming style with which we associate the shark, but out of the water it is severely strained. A shark can be crushed to death by its own weight.

Because cartilage precedes bone in skeletal development—cartilage turning into bone through ossification—it was at one time believed that fish may have been an evolutionary outgrowth of sharks. This enhanced the idea that the shark was a "primitive," unevolved fish, unchanged from the dawn of creation. Actually, the bony fish predated the arrival of the shark and developed quite independently of it. At any rate, the advantage of a cartilaginous skeleton is a lighter and more flexible frame, and is necessary to sharks' survival. Because sharks do not have the gas-filled swim bladder of fish, they must have as minimally dense a body as possible in order to move freely in the water. Their oily livers keep their buoyancy neutral. In other words, while the shark will sink if it stops swimming, it can also propel its low-density body with very little effort. The typical pelagic shark weighs in water only a fraction of what it weighs in air. However, sharks that live primarily on the sea bottom, and have less need of lift in the water—species such as the genus *Squatina*, the angel sharks—are considerably more dense in water.

The skin of the shark is also different from most fish. Instead of scales, sharks have denticles—small, hard, stud-like protuberances containing nerve and blood vessels. These denticles, as the name implies, are made from the same material as the shark's teeth. They are curved and rough at the rear edge. Rub the shark's skin from front to back and the feeling is smooth, rub it from back to front and there is a painful feeling of sharp bristles. It is easy to be injured by a shark in this way, even if one is not subject to direct attack.

It is not known for sure if these prickly spines are for protection or if they have some hydrodynamic purpose, helping the shark move more smoothly through the water. There are also variant skin textures among different species. The bullhead shark of the family Heterodontidae lacks the sharp spines, while on the prickly dogfish (*Oxynotus bruniensis*), the spines are sharper than average—petting one would be like stroking your hand across barbed wire.

The muscles in the shark's body are attached to the skin instead of the skeleton, which allows for more variable and precise locomotion among "typical" sharks—by which we mean any of the streamlined, predatory sharks, including the whaler (or requiem). The structure of the muscles enables the shark to maintain a casual cruising speed, rippling along using its whole form to propel itself. But if sudden speed and strength are needed, the shark can stiffen skin against muscle, the tail alone waving, shooting it forward at great speed, a virtual torpedo. The requiem shark is built to move with speed and efficiency when needed, its fins giving it a highly-tuned ability to accelerate, turn, twist, roll and brake.

Bottom-dwelling sharks have little need for locomotive virtuosity, and so the tail fin of a species such as the carpet shark is underdeveloped. By contrast, the modifications on the caudal fin of the mackerel shark, with its reduced upper lobe and strong caudal keels, help make it perhaps the fastest swimmer of all sharks. A mackerel shark, such as *Carcharodon carcharias*, or the great white shark, has a tail—or caudal—fin with equally large upper and lower lobes, designed to meet its need for a slow, steady cruising speed, as well as high speed bursts for attacking prey.

Actually, the shape of the tails varies greatly from species to species, adapting to its particular nature, and the peculiarities of shark tails do not have only to do with swimming ability. The thresher shark's long, scimitar-like upper lobe is used to "herd" its prey of smaller fish and squid, and the mitten-like tail of the cookiecutter shark appears to attract prey with its strange luminescence.

While the caudal fin does the propulsive work, the pectoral fins on the sides near the center of the body keep the shark's balance, along with the smaller dorsal, pelvic and anal fins. For many people, the dorsal fin (located at top center) is frighteningly emblematic of the "man-eating shark"—the dark, streamlined crescent knifing through the surface of the water. Again, as with the tail, the other fins show modifications (though generally less extreme) from species to species.

Sharks have even greater diversity in their head shapes, none more so than the genus *Sphyrna*, or the hammerhead sharks. Its head is shaped laterally, with its eyes placed far apart on the ends of the left and right stalks. An even more extreme variation of the hammerhead is the winghead shark, with its wide, hammerlike head fully half the size of its entire body. A lesser-known oddity is the sawshark. Its head ends in a long tapered snout covered with upraised denticles like the teeth of a saw. Not surprisingly, the "saw" is used as a weapon against prey. The horn shark has peculiarly piggish nostrils, while the flat head of the angel shark is more reminiscent of a ray, and the obscure goblin shark is an *Alien*-like gargoyle with protruding jaw and dagger snout.

The placement of the shark's mouth on the underside of the head is curious, as it is logical for the bottom-feeding species but not for the swimming predators, which attack their prey straight on. Scientists believe that there was a period, starting perhaps 300 million years ago, when all sharks were bottom-feeders, living on molluscs and crustaceans. With an increase in the swimming fish population, some species of shark evolved to become predators, although the mouths remained below the heads on these sharks. Early, badly-researched reports on sharks had it that they were unable to bite at anything in front of them, and even that they were forced to turn upside-down to feed. In fact, the design of the shark's mouth is much more sophisticated and, in some circumstances, frightening. The shark cannot see what it is about to bite directly in front of it, true, but its nostrils and electroreceptors on the snout deliver necessary sensory information. (More about these later.) Sharks can indeed *bite* at what is in front of them: the protruding snout actually rises back while the jaws are thrown forward, teeth fully exposed.

Those jaws, those teeth embody much of the mythology of terror that man has directed at the shark. And to be sure, the shark's jaws and teeth are super-efficient machinery that have made the bigger species apex predators, the top of the food chain.

The design of the jaw in the modern shark is nothing short of amazing. Its mobility comes from its not being bound to the braincase, allowing the jaws to protrude during an attack and feeding. In an attack, the shark's head rises so that the jaw extends outward. With large prey, the shark's lower jaw hits first, holding the prey in place as the upper jaw comes forward and down, teeth digging in as the shark's head shakes violently, effectively sawing a chunk out of the prey and then tearing it away. The force of a shark's bite is tremendous—estimated at 20 tons per square inch for an eight-footer. To withstand the force of impact, the shark itself comes equipped with "shock absorbers," expanded dorsal and ventral processes which protect the spine.

The great strength of the jaws would be meaningless if they did not contain equally deadly teeth. Here again are found detailed and subtle designs, with teeth made to match the characteristic prey of a given shark. The great white shark has wide, serrated teeth made for biting out large chunks of its prey. Other sharks (such as the mako, which swallows small fish whole for its diet) have thin, sharply-pointed teeth used for impaling the fish. The bottom-dwelling swellshark, on the other hand, feeds on hard-shelled crustaceans, for which purpose it has small, sharp teeth.

The shape of the teeth will also vary according to the age of a particular species. Young great whites, not so likely to take on a more mature white's large prey, have the narrower, pointier teeth designed for impaling small fish.

Sharks, unlike humans, have no fear of losing a tooth. Large predators in particular blunt or break many teeth in the course of feeding, but each damaged tooth is quickly replaced by a new one. Sharks come equipped with an almost endless supply of new teeth, which grow in rows along a membrane known as a tooth bed. These "reserve teeth" simply move out into place as they are needed, thousands in a shark's lifetime.

Another long-held theory about sharks was that they had poor eyesight. Once again, much of the early research has been proven ignorant. The eyes of sharks have much variation and some remarkable capacities. Generally, active swimming predators have larger eyes, while the less active, native to shallow water, like those of the genus *Heterodontus*, the horn shark, have smaller eyes. On most sharks, the eyelids do not move, but some have a membrane that will cover and protect the eye during feeding. The reason the shark does not need an eyelid is because the pupil itself is able to control the amount of light coming in. Behind the retina of the shark's eye is a tapetum, or mirror-like plates that reflect light into the eye's receptor cells, increasing sensitivity. Such complex visual equipment proves that the shark's eyesight is not as poor or as simple as was once believed.

But the eyes are just one component in the shark's elaborate sensory system. The hearing of most sharks is very well-developed. Although ear openings are small, sharks can hear very slight sounds and water movements, and can pick up low frequency noises unheard by man. Scientists have shown how they can quickly summon sharks by creating pulse tones similar to that of an injured fish. The shark's sense of smell is also well-developed. Experiments have shown that sharks can smell prey from great distances, even when no other sensory stimulus is involved. The olfactory sacs in the nostrils are very sensitive, constantly "testing" the water for odors. These nasal sacs have an entrance and exit for the tested water, allowing a constant fresh flow. It takes just a thousandth of a second for the shark's sense of smell to react to stimuli, and the amount of that stimuli in the water may be infinitesimal.

The shark's most intriguing sensory power—and the one most alien to man—involves electricity. Through small organs on its head, called the ampullae of Lorenzini, the shark is able to detect electrical signals. This electroreceptor system may be used in connection with the earth's magnetic field, aiding the shark in navigation, but its primary use is probably as a kind of short-range radar for finding prey, i.e., detecting the presence of camouflaged or hidden fish. Also, in the moment of attack, with its snout raised and its eyes rolling back or covered for protection, the shark's electric detectors will "tune in" on the prey's electro-field. Scientists have found that when sharks have seemingly attacked inanimate objects like boats and shark cages in baited water, it is not out of some savage urge to eat *anything* but due instead to the strange and confusing electric signals surrounding the bait. Under ordinary conditions, the shark makes extraordinarily effective use of its whole elaborate and interconnecting sensory system.

Sharks differ again from ordinary fish in their method of reproduction. The majority of fish species lay countless eggs into the water to be fertilized there. It is a lengthy and haphazard method, with most of the eggs eaten by other fish long before they are born. By contrast, the shark bears far fewer young, yet provides far more protection for their survival.

Fertilization among sharks is done internally. Sexual intercourse involves the male shark inserting his penis-like appendage called a "clasper" into the female's reproductive opening, the cloaca. The courtship rites can be painful for the female, who is often viciously bitten on the body and fins by her mate before copulation. It is probably for this reason that the denticles on female sharks of some species are much thicker than those of the male.

There are three methods employed by sharks in developing their young. They will either lay eggs just as fish do (the oviparous method), or hatch eggs inside the mother (the ovoviviparous method) or else create a placental connection with the mother (the viviparous method). In the first—the oviparous method—the embryonic shark is contained in a resilient egg case. These cases come in an array of shapes, such as the bullhead shark's corkscrew or the purse-shaped case of the swellshark. The cases are laid on the sea floor, screwed into crevices or tangled in seaweed, where they are protected from the buffeting of currents and hidden from potential predators. Some egg capsules come equipped with little string attachments that knot in the coral. Inside the egg case is the embryo and a yolk from which it feeds. The yolk shrinks as the shark grows until finally the hatchling is ready to crawl out of the case and into the water. The empty egg cases of sharks often wash up on the beach, where children collect them as they do seashells.

In the more common ovoviviparous and viviparous methods, sharks produce live young. The former procedure involves an egg growing within the uterus of the mother, where it hatches. In vivipary, the egg is nurtured directly by the mother through a placenta. Gestation period for a pregnant shark can range from a few months to nearly two years. Offspring are born quite large in some cases, as in the five-foot-long newborn basking shark (*Cetorhinus maximus*). The newborn is an almost perfect miniature of the parent, and immediately begins to swim and search for food.

With their varied methods of birth, sharks also have diverse breeding cycles. Some sharks breed yearly, in any month, others only at certain months of the year. The females of some species take a year's vacation between each birthing cycle. The lemon shark (*Negaprion brevirostris*), for example, after its year-long pregnancy, will not reproduce again for two years.

Much is still unknown about reproduction and breeding among sharks. Many major species have never been observed copulating or giving birth.

Much of what we do know about sharks, their biology and habits, is only recently learned, and often contradicts some of the most basic theories about these fish. Take, for example, the mystery of the "sleeping sharks." Sharks "breathe" by extracting oxygen from the water that flows through their gills. Active ocean-going species use a process of "ram-jet respiration," pushing water through their gills as they swim forward. Scientists believed that these sharks— including most of the well-known large predators—could never stop swimming or they would die. It was not until the mid-1970s that science discovered how some sharks had overcome this wearying condition.

Divers in the Caribbean waters near Mexico's Isla Mujeres came upon caves in which dangerous requiem sharks were lying about in a state of lethargy. The sharks remained in place and unfrightened even when divers touched them. It was such an unusual sight that at first the divers believed the sharks were all dead or dying, that they had come upon a kind of secret "sharks' graveyard." Shark experts came to investigate, and after much testing, it was found that there was freshwater seepage in the caves. This environment not only seemed to help loosen parasites that clung to the sharks but, more importantly, the high oxygen content in the caves allowed the sharks to breathe without movement. Furthermore, the water in the caves seemed to have a pleasurable tranquilizing effect on the sharks. Their defenses dropped; the resting—if not exactly sleeping—sharks would sit in the caves, seemingly daydreaming as remoras—those sucker fish often found attached to sharks—went about encircling them, picking off parasites. The sharks' use of the caves as part-dormitory, part-cleaning station (and part "opium den," as some would have it), left marine biologists speechless. There was, and is, still much more to be learned about the habits of these fascinating creatures.

The "Clan" of the Shark

The 350 known species of sharks are divided into 8 different orders:

Order Squatiniformes. One family of raylike sharks, all similar versions of the *Squatina squatina*, or the angel shark. These sharks are bottom-dwellers, common to the continental shelves.

Order Pristiophoriformes. Another highly distinctive family, including five variations on the sawshark, a shark with a long, saw-like snout. The single family belonging to this order is bottom-dwelling and lives at medium depths in the Atlantic, the Pacific and the Indian Oceans.

Order Hexanchiformes. Two families make up this order. The eel-shaped frilled shark (*Chlamydoselachus anguineus*) gets its name from the frilly covering on its gill openings. It is found on continental shelves throughout the world. The sixgill and sevengill sharks come equipped—as their name describes—with one or two extra gill slits. They are found in coastal and offshore waters.

Order Heterodontiformes. Comprised of one family, the bullhead sharks. Distinguished by the combination of fin spines on the dorsal and anal fins.

Order Squaliformes. There are three families and 82 species in this order, also referred to as the dogfish sharks. Dogfish sharks are found in all the seas of the world, and may have the widest range of any shark . They come in an equally wide range of sizes, from the very large (the Greenland shark, or *Somniosus microcephalus*, reaching lengths of 20 feet) to the very small (the cookiecutter, or *Isistius brasiliensis*, under a foot in length).

Order Carcharhiniformes. This order alone has nearly 200 species, over half of all known species of shark. Also known as the groundsharks, they tend to have longish snouts and long mouths. With so many species, the Carcharhiniformes naturally cover a wide assortment of sizes and habitats in the eight families comprising the order (houndsharks, barbeled houndsharks, catsharks, false catsharks, finback catsharks, weasel sharks, hammerhead sharks, and requiem sharks). The requiem sharks are made up of several species with the "classic" shark profile—such as the tiger, the blue and the grey reef. An alternate term for the requiem sharks—whaler—derives from their having attacked the catch of whaling ships.

Order Orectolobiformes. The seven families in this order represent much diversity, from the splotchy-patterned, bottom-dwelling wobbegong, to the huge and glorious whale shark, the largest fish in the world (the whale itself, needless to say, a mammal). The whale shark is one of only three filter-feeders in the shark world (ingesting huge quantities of plankton as it swims), but most other carpetsharks, as Orectolobiformes are also known, have a diet of bottom fish, crustaceans, bivalves, etc. This knowledge, however, is only presumed in the case of the collared and longtailed carpetsharks, about which there is little or no dietary data.

Order Lamniformes. The seven families in this order, also known as mackerel sharks, include one each of the ugliest, the newest, and the most notorious. The goblin shark (*Mitsukurina owstoni*) has a grotesque and frightening face and dwells on the sea floor but little else is known about it. Even less well-known is the recently-discovered megamouth (*Megachasma pelagios*). There are only three specimens to date, the first having been caught when it swallowed a ship's anchor. Like the whale shark and basking shark (another Lamniforme or mackerel shark), megamouth is a filter feeder. Most notorious of the order is *Carcharodon carcharias*, the man-eater of legend (and it is often more legend than fact), the great white shark.

The number of species in a particular shark family may be as many as 92 or more (the various described and undescribed species of catsharks) or as few as one (several families of a single unique species such as *Rhiniodon typus*, the whale shark). The classification of some sharks is subject to change as scientists uncover more information about them. And there may be additions to a family as new species are discovered. In just the last two decades, the number of known shark species has nearly doubled and shark researchers have no doubts that more discoveries are on the way.

Life on the floor of the deepest seas remains a particular mystery. In this dark, distant world, there may be sharks with shapes and characteristics yet unimaginable. For some shark researchers, the prospect is daunting—little enough is known about the hundreds of species already classified. In the past (and perhaps at present) many species have been confusingly or wrongly named. The same species found at different parts of the world will end up with two different names. Most of these mix-ups are finally being sorted out as worldwide marine scientists work together to compile a standard taxonomy for sharks. The work is not easy, since much of it must be done in difficult and perilous conditions. Sharks have proven to be very difficult to study in captivity. Only a handful of species have been able to thrive for more than a few months outside their natural environment. Transporting the animals is a major problem, and once they reach the aquaria or other locations, the sharks tend to stop eating and die.

Sharks are found in every part of the world, from tropical to arctic regions. They are found in shallow water and in the bottomless depths of mid-ocean. They come in the sleek, streamlined shape of the classic requiem shark, and in strange shapes that nearly defy description. They are as colossal as

SHARKS:

By Order and Family

The 350 known species of sharks fall into 30 different shark families, and these are divided among eight different *orders*.

ORDER SQUATINIFORMES
Family Squatinidae . . . . Angel Sharks

ORDER PRISTIOPHORIFORMES
Family Pristiophoridae . . . . Sawsharks

ORDER HEXANCHIFORMES
Family Chlamydoselachidae . . . . . Frilled Sharks
Family Hexanchidae . . . . Sixgill and Sevengill Sharks

ORDER HETERODONTIFORMES
Family Heterodontidae . . . . Bullhead Sharks

ORDER SQUALIFORMES
Family Squalidae . . . . Dogfish Sharks
Family Oxynotidae . . . . Roughsharks
Family Echinorhinidae . . . . Bramble Sharks

ORDER CARCHARHINIFORMES
Family Proscylliidae . . . . Finback Catsharks
Family Sphyrnidae . . . . Hammerhead Sharks
Family Hemigaleidae . . . . Weasel Sharks
Family Scyliorhinidae . . . . Catsharks
Family Pseudotriakidae . . . . False Catsharks
Family Triakidae . . . . Houndsharks
Family Leptochariidae . . . . Barbled Houndsharks
Family Carcharhinididae . . . . . . Requiem Sharks

ORDER ORECTOLOBIFORMES
Family Orectolobidae . . . . Wobbegongs
Family Parascylliidae . . . . Collared Carpetsharks
Family Brachaeluridae . . . . Blind Sharks
Family Rhiniodontidae . . . . Whale Sharks
Family Stegostomatidae . . . . Zebra Sharks
Family Ginglymostomatidae . . . . Nurse Sharks
Family Hemiscylliidae . . . . Longtailed Carpetsharks

ORDER LAMNIFORMES
Family Cetorhinidae . . . . Basking Sharks
Family Mitsukurinidae . . . . Goblin Sharks
Family Odontaspididae . . . . Sand Tiger Sharks
Family Megachasmidae . . . . Megamouth Sharks
Family Pseudocarchariidae . . . . . Crocodile Sharks
Family Lamnidae . . . . Mackerel Sharks
Family Alopiidae . . . . Thresher Sharks

Rhiniodon typus, the great whale shark, and as tiny as *Etmopterus lucifer*, the foot-long "devil shark." They can be man-eaters, but many more are docile and harmless to humans. With 350 different species of sharks, we could not hope to describe all of them in one volume, but some of the 350—some of the most interesting, unusual or dangerous—deserve a closer look.

Great White Shark

Carcharodon carcharias, or the great white shark, has also been known as "White Death." It is the shark with the worst reputation for savagery, the giant apex predator that has attacked and killed humans, seemingly without provocation. It is the giant predatory beast of legend with its enormous jaws, and terrifying teeth—long, sharp, serrated daggers, perfectly designed for tearing off chunks of flesh. It has been mythologized as a "killing machine," ever on the hunt for prey. And stories of this shark's voraciousness are not exaggerated. Great whites as small as 10 feet have been captured, opened up, and found to contain a whole sea lion. The carcass of another smallish great white contained a man six-feet tall. Imagine what a 20-foot specimen would be capable of swallowing.

For all of the attention and legend attached to the great white shark as a man-eater, there have actually been relatively few attacks proven to be the work of this species. Of those attacks accurately ascribed to the great white, most are not fatal. Off the coast of California, where these sharks are common, there have been only four fatalities in the last 30 years. Many people who have been attacked were bitten once and then the shark turned away. The shark may be only defending itself, as the powerful jaws of the white shark could undoubtedly kill just about anything if such was its goal.

Often, the great white is given credit—discredit, really—for attacks on humans out of pure ignorance. Many attacks take place in the warm waters of the tropics, where great whites are seldom found. Yet, as the most famous of pelagic predators, it is blamed. The attacks are probably perpetrated by any of the aggressive sharks common to the tropics, such as the bull shark (*Carcharhinus leucas*).

How large do great whites get? Many have been caught in the 18-foot range and it is likely they can grow to over 20 feet-long. But reports of seeing great whites of 40 feet and more are probably pure fantasy.

Like most open ocean predators, the great white shark is not a picky eater. In the wilds of the ocean, food is never in great abundance and the great white feeds when it can. It is not intimidated by creatures its own size and eagerly devours large mammals, seals, sea lions, turtles and other sharks. For all its reputation, however, the great white will sometimes go out of his way to avoid an encounter with man. Many attacks on humans are thought to have occurred because the shark mistook people for its favorite food, sea lions.

Hammerhead Sharks

The genus *Sphyrna*, or hammerheads, is the most easily recognizable of all sharks. The body is quite ordinary and could be any one of several species, but no one could mistake its bizarre head—the lateral-shaped stalk with an eerie eye at each end. It is thought that the peculiar shape aids the shark's movement in the water, acting as a forward planing surface. The hammerhead *is* an extremely maneuverable creature. But, the truth be known, there is as yet no real logical explanation for the extreme body modifications of this species.

If the hammer-shaped head and separated eyes help the shark's movements, they certainly hinder them as well. With the eyes located far apart on the stalk, the hammerhead shark must continually twist its head from side to side in order to see forward. Divers are able to identify an approaching hammerhead from this movement, even before the distinctive hammer-shape becomes visible.

There are nine species of hammerhead, including the scalloped, the great, and the winghead. The head of the hammerhead shark is five times as wide as it is long and is quite flat. The winghead, *Eusphyra blochii*, is the most extreme version of the type, with its head width averaging half the size of its body length. Some hammerheads are small, three feet or so, but the largest grow to 15 feet. Hammerheads are found in coastal and offshore waters in all tropic and temperate areas. The hammerhead is hunted for its liver, which is unusually large and filled with oil—a great source of Vitamin A.

For a long while, it was assumed that sharks did not swim in schools. Then divers witnessed an amazing phenomenon at the El Bajo seamount in the Sea of Cortez, Baja California. Large groups—200 and more—of scalloped hammerheads (*Sphyrna lewini*) congregated there regularly. This congregation is one more unique occurrence in the world of sharks that science cannot yet explain. Perhaps the gatherings have to do with mating, though there is no strong evidence of it as yet. Films of these gatherings, with the hundreds of strange-shaped heads swimming by in formation, have the feeling of a surrealist dream.

Whale Shark

Rhiniodon typus, or the whale shark, is the largest fish in the sea. A shark the size of 45-feet is not unusual, and there have been confirmed sightings of 60-footers. Marine biologists believe even larger ones may exist.

The whale shark was unknown to man before 1828 and none were photographed until Hans Hass shot film of a 26-foot-long specimen in the 1950s. Although it may have been taken for a whale by sailors, it is a true shark. For all its length and broad body, the whale shark actually moves with grace, powered along by the effortless-seeming movements of its huge and powerful tail. Divers coming upon the gentle creature have been known to hitch a ride, but one must beware of the tail, for an unexpected slap can cause serious injury.

The whale shark is a benign giant, posing no threat of attack. It is—along with the basking shark and the megamouth—a filter feeder. It collects its diet of marine organisms by swimming through them at two or three miles per hour with its mouth open. While the whale shark can be the size of a city bus, the plankton on which it feeds are individually no larger than a thumbnail. It will occasionally supplement its planktonic diet by rising up vertically through a school of tuna or other fish, swallowing them as it surfaces.

The whale shark has a uniquely beautiful pattern to its skin, shades of blue in circles and vertical lines. Rarely seen, a diver who encounters the whale shark does not soon forget it.

Grey Reef Shark

The grey reef shark, or *Carcharhinus amblyrhynchos*, is a classic requiem shark. It is a major predator along the coral reefs of the Indo-Pacific and the Red Sea, a predator of great speed and maneuverability with its streamlined, torpedo-like body. It is not a large shark, averaging only about five feet in length. The grey reef shark often hunts along promontories on the reef where the current is strongest and where there is a great concentration of food.

Though not as well known as the great white, the grey reef has an almost equal reputation for aggressive behavior. It is this shark that often figures in tales of "feeding frenzies." There are differing opinions on what triggers the frenzy: a single drop of blood, fear of competition or merely the agitating vibrations of the first shark to feed. At any rate, anywhere in the vicinity of a grey reef is no place to be once a frenzy begins.

Another example of the grey reef's aggression is seen during mating. A vicious courtship dance is performed, the female grey reef shark swimming off by herself only to have her prospective mate approach with sudden violence, biting the female about the body and fins several times before copulating with her. The male's "love bites" may leave severe gouges in the female.

The grey reef is also known for its distinctive "dangerous threat" display. The shark will react to a threatening diver with this show of imminent danger. The shark begins by turning figure eights or small circles, the head swaying from side to side, then hunches its back, lowering its pectoral fins and holding its mouth open. Frozen in this position, the shark will begin to sink for a moment before snapping into terrifying action, attacking the perceived antagonist with its deadly bite.

And yet, for all these shows of violence and unpredictability, grey reef sharks can act quite benign. Divers have, in fact, trained grey reefs to be fed by hand. One diver in the Maldives has been photographed feeding the grey reef fish held in his own mouth.

Blue Shark

Prionace glauca, the blue shark, is a requiem shark of the family Carcharhinididae, the family responsible for most of the attacks on humans. Yet many divers consider the blue to be unaggressive, easily fended off with a hit or shove. Make no mistake, however, the blue shark is capable of becoming excited and aggressive.

The blue is stimulated to attack by the presence of blood in the water. It has been known to attack the victims of shipwrecks and plane crashes in open ocean, and many men and women have survived a terrible air or sea disaster only to be killed by an agitated blue shark. Nevertheless, this species prefers a diet of squid to that of man. When it comes upon a concentration of this fish it will charge back and forth through them, mouth wide open, swallowing as many as it can. When the shark cannot fit any more squid into its body, it will vomit to make room and then continue feeding.

The long pectoral fins of the blue shark allow it to swim gracefully slow, but it is capable of sudden, short bursts of speed. The blue travels widely but prefers cool water temperatures. In temperate waters it will swim close to the surface, but in the tropics it stays at greater depths where the water is cooler. In summer, off the coast of California, blue sharks practice sexual segregation. The males stay to the south in warmer waters, while the females go to the colder north.

Tiger Shark

Galeocerdo cuvier, or the tiger shark, is one of the most feared creatures on land or sea, and with good reason. It can be a ferocious predator. With its big head and blunt snout, the tiger shark cuts a harsh and threatening figure. It gets its name from the stripes marking the body, but it would be equally well named for its personality.

Tigers are large sharks. They have been reported at lengths in excess of 17 feet and often cruise well-touristed beaches for food. Tigers are found off the southern coasts of the United States and will feed in very shallow water, making them a serious threat to swimmers.

The tiger shark will eat almost anything: large carrion (such as pigs and cows), sea birds perching on the water's surface, other sharks, and human beings. The design of the tiger shark's teeth allows it a wide selection of foods. It can impale its prey on the sharpened apex of the tooth and then chop it to pieces with the serrated edges below the apex. A bite from a tiger shark leaves a distinctively curved wound.

Angel Shark

The form of the angel shark (genus *Squatina*) is highly distinctive, looking unlike any traditional shark and more like a manta ray. Like the ray, the angel shark's body and pectoral fins are flat, its muscle and skeleton are dense, and it swims by making vertical waves across its flattened fins. Unlike the ray, the angel shark's pectoral fins are not attached to its head.

The angel shark is found in cool temperate waters along the continental shelves. It is a bottom-dweller and feeds from the sea floor, a diet of crustaceans, molluscs, bivalves, and sea snails. It is an "ambush predator," hiding in the sand, ready to pounce on any small fish that comes near. The angel shark's sandy color and pebble-like markings serve as camouflage. It is a most sedentary predator, and will sit motionless on the ocean floor until something comes close.

Bull Shark

Carcharhinus leucas, or the bull shark, is suitably named, with its thick, heavy body. It grows to over 12 feet in tropical and sub-tropical waters around the world. It has small eyes and razor-sharp teeth. The bull will swallow smaller prey whole, but when attacking something larger—which it will do quite fearlessly—its teeth are used to tear out numerous cylinders of flesh. Although it has none of the notoriety of the great white or tiger shark, the bull shark—which often feeds in shallow water near beaches—is responsible for many human deaths. The most unusual characteristic of the bull shark is that it will enter freshwater lakes and rivers and will stay there for weeks at a time. It may travel deep within bodies of fresh water in Africa and Central and South America. Bull sharks have been found in the Amazon River more than 2,000 miles from the sea.

Horn Shark

The horn shark is readily identifiable, but for three different physical attributes. It is instantly identifiable by its distinctive snout, resembling that of a pig, and it is commonly called the "pig shark" for this reason. It gets the name "horn shark," however, for the horn-like spines on its dorsal fins. Furthermore, the horn is interesting enough to merit a third descriptive name—

Heterodontus—its family name meaning "different teeth," so-called because of the combined cutting and cobbled crushing teeth peculiar to this group.

The horn shark is found in the Pacific and Indian Oceans, roaming from shallow waters to depths of several hundred meters. It is a bottom-dweller, and feeds on a diet of crustaceans, sea urchins, gastropods and some bony fish. This shark moves only as much and as often as absolutely necessary. It prefers to sit and wait for its prey, hiding in caves, gullies and under beds of kelp, waiting for some small creature to crawl by. Still in hiding, it may spend all day at rest. The horn shark may grow to only three feet at maturity and, as a shark group, is not considered a threat to man.

Because it moves so little, the distribution of the horn shark is obviously limited. Its whole life may be spent in one small area of the sea or an archipelago.

Nurse Shark

The nurse shark, member of the family Ginglymostomatidae, is another species with distinctively modified features. The nurse appears to have two long, extended "fangs," but these are actually twin barbels on the snout. They are fleshy, not hard, and are there to provide the nurse shark with a sense of touch.

The nurse is an unaggressive creature. It is lazy and peaceful, spending much of its time resting on the sea floor. It moves about mainly at night, on a search for food. It has small, strong teeth designed for cracking the shells of molluscs. Its most creative method of feeding involves the use of its pharyngeal cavity to create a suction pressure that will suck small prey from between rocks.

Swellshark

The swellshark, a member of the family Scyliorhinidae, dwells on the ocean floor the entire day, moving only in order to feed itself—and even then not making a strenuous job of it. The swellshark will open its huge mouth so wide as it moves that fish will mistakenly swim inside. It prefers a diet of crustaceans and small fish and, at an average length of less than four feet, it is not a real threat to humans, despite rows of razor-sharp teeth.

The swellshark gets its name from an ability to pump itself up with water or air, swelling it like a balloon. This strange behavior is actually a defensive mechanism. The frightened swellshark will blow itself up within a rock crevice or some other narrow hiding place, making it immovable and uneatable.

The swellshark's method of producing young is worth particular attention. The embryo is attached to a nourishing egg yolk which gradually disappears as the baby shark feeds on it and grows. This embryo is contained within a golden- hued egg case. These cases

are an amazing phenomenon of nature, a sturdy container that comes with strings which attach to seaweed, kelp or coral, holding the case in place. After nearly a year, the egg case will split and the baby shark will emerge. On the back of the hatchling are two rows of oversized denticles which act as a ratchet, helping to force the shark out of the case. As soon as the swellshark gets out of the egg case, it begins to swim and hunt for food.

Man-Eaters and Man

What can be said with some certainty is that very few sharks are ordinarily dangerous to man. Out of the hundreds of species perhaps 10 or a dozen have been known to attack man without provocation. These include the great white and assorted members of the requiem shark family (tiger shark, blue shark, bull, grey reef). Without a doubt, these sharks have perpetrated some horrible attacks on humans. Bathers, divers, shipwreck victims have been bitten and gouged severely, had limbs torn from their bodies, and have been swallowed nearly whole. But the number of these incidents is tiny in proportion to the worldwide "shark attack" hysteria that has so often erupted. In Australia, for instance, where the long coastline hosts numerous large predators including the great white, the beaches are considered among the world's most dangerous because of shark attacks. Yet 90 years of record-keeping show only a few hundred shark attacks and 100 fatalities. Of course, one such incident is one too many, but it was discovered that nearly as many serious *dog* attacks had occurred in the same period, and the number of fatalities in car accidents was, of course, much higher.

A majority of attacks occur at bathing beaches mainly because this is where large groups of people are gathered. The attacking shark may actually be in its own natural feeding territory. It may not only be hungry but agitated by the noise and thrashing in the water. If the species of shark does not normally feed on larger fish, the attack may only be out of fright. Most attacks involve the shark taking a bite out of the victim and then moving away. If, however, the shark is an apex predator, used to feeding with no size limitations, it may attack and devour a human. But sharks with a taste for human flesh, deliberately seeking out human prey, is, so far as is known, pure fiction.

Some incidents of shark bites that make it into the attack tables do not even take place in water. Fishermen often land a shark which they believe to be stunned or dead, only to have the fish revive and snap off a few fingers. Other incidents involve divers ignorantly or irresponsibly goading a shark into attack by petting it, chasing it, or trying to ride it. Ordinarily sluggish and peaceful sharks like the nurse shark will turn around and murder a diver if they are sufficiently harassed. The nurse shark's teeth are not made for slashing bites, but it will crush the diver between its jaws and hold him until he drowns. At other times, divers will attempt to hand-feed fish to some relatively passive species of shark. Such situations can suddenly get out of hand, turning into a feeding frenzy in which the diver may end up as part of the chaotic meal. Some shark bites happen each year when a bather accidentally puts his foot down on a bottom-dwelling shark. The number of these "provoked" attacks, as they are officially labeled, is far greater than the unprovoked.

Confirmed man-eaters, luckily for all who ever enter the sea, are relatively few in number. Even these species can be peaceful or standoffish, but there is no denying their aggressive, lethal capabilities. The tiger shark (*Galeocerdo cuvier*) and the bull shark (*Carcharhinus leucas*) are both voracious predators and scavengers, known to eat almost anything. Encounters with humans occur in shallow water, sometimes in less than three feet of water. Some people have had the misfortune to encounter the bull shark deep within freshwater lakes and rivers—it is the only shark known for this. The tiger shark's jagged teeth leave highly distinctive crescent wounds, while the bull's razor-like teeth with cut circles of flesh out of its prey. Some man-eaters seldom see man—deepwater species like the blue (*Prionace glauca*) and the oceanic whitetip (*Carcharhinus longimanus*). When they do encounter humans at sea—the victims of air and sea disasters—the results are often horrifying.

The most dangerous—certainly the most famous—of man-eaters is the great white shark. Great whites have taken sizable chunks out of boats and surf boards as well as humans. Scientists believe most of these attacks are due to confusion on the shark's part—it may think the objects are large sea mammals, one of its favorite foods. The great white seldom actually eats its human victims. It will often take a vicious bite and then circle around as the victim dies.

The descriptions above may make it difficult to sympathize with sharks, but, terrifying as such encounters may be, they are extremely rare and represent the behavior of only a fraction of the varied species of sharks. But even among confirmed man-eaters, most attacks occur when man has invaded and disturbed the shark's natural habitat—and man has not had a reputation for respecting the territorial rights of any species, including his own.

In point of fact, the shark is in more danger from us than we are from it. About 50 men and women are killed by sharks each year worldwide. In that same year, man kills—for food, sport or "thrills"—approximately 100 million sharks. This slaughter has already begun to bring some species of shark close to extinction. But a fish with such a notorious reputation as the shark's often has trouble receiving the kind of national and international protection offered to other endangered or over-hunted animals. Perhaps, though, as more people begin to understand the unique and beautiful attributes of the shark, and put its predatory nature into realistic perspective, something will be done, before it is too late.

Its face stained with blood, a great white shark shows the smile that has sent shivers down many a spine. The teeth of the great white are triangular and serrated, excellent for rending the flesh of prey both small and large.

Sharks do not have the gas-filled swim bladder of bony fishes, which was once considered a detriment to their efficiency as swimmers. But, in fact, many sharks are better equipped to dive or climb up through the water because their neutral buoyancy is not controlled by changing water pressure.

When divorced from its bad reputation, the great white shark (Carcharodon carcharias) can be seen as the magnificent creature it is. The design of the body is hydrodynamic perfection, built for a lifetime of effortless cruising.

Far from a simple, fierce "killing machine" as myth would have it, the great white—here seen off the South Australian coast—is a creature of great intelligence as well as savagery.

The eyes of the pelagic—or oceanic—blue shark have a layer of reflective cells passing light from the retina to receptor cells.

The gracefully slow-moving blue shark (Prionace glauca). Like many sharks, the blue shark is more adapted to sprinting than sustaining a rapid rate; it has also been demonstrated that they use ocean currents in order to travel far.

The blue shark is stimulated by blood, and is known to attack victims of ocean shipwrecks and plane crashes. Many men and women have survived a terrible air or sea disaster only to be killed by an agitated blue.

*The massive face of a whale shark
(Rhiniodon typus). The
immensity of this fish is indicated
by the size of the two divers
hovering behind it.*

In Baja California, divers came
up upon this 40-foot-long
whale shark. Rarely seen, an
encounter with a whale shark is
not soon forgotten.

The hammerhead is perhaps the strongest swimmer of all sharks, although its movements—throwing its head from side to side—may be regarded by some as ungainly. The hammerhead moves this way in order to see, as its eyes are located on either side of its head.

As a predator, the grey reef shark (Carcharhinus amblyrhynchos) *has speed and maneuverability on its side. In sizes that range from five to six-and-a-half feet-long, the grey reef is considered a more fierce competitor than the whitetip reef shark.*

As its name implies, it is on the reef that the grey reef shark can most often be found. They often congregate where strong ocean currents bring the largest concentration of prey together.

The whitetip reef shark (Triaenodon óbesus) *can be found along the coral reefs of the Indian Ocean and the South Pacific. It rests in crevices or on the reef floor by day, looking for food only at night.*

An oceanic whitetip shark, or Carcharhinus longimanus.
These sharks are a species of requiem shark and stay in
deep water. Under ordinary circumstances they are unlikely
to encounter humans. But they are known to attack and
devour shipwreck and air crash victims adrift in mid-ocean.

A *blacktip, or* Carcharhinus limbatus, *with its odd splash of black at the tip of its fin. The blacktip shark is said to defer to silvertip and to Galapagos sharks when either are present, due to a little-known but complex social hierarchy.*

A leopard shark, or Triakis semifasciata, *resting on the sea bottom. The leopard, with its diet of small foods, poses little threat to humans.*

While it is a largely unaggressive species, the nurse shark
will attack if threatened. It has small, strong teeth designed
for cracking the shells of molluscs. Its more unusual method of
feeding involves the use of its pharyngeal cavity to create a suction
pressure that will suck small prey from between rocks.

With its big head and blunt snout,
the tiger shark (Galeocerdo cuvier) cuts a
harsh and threatening figure. It gets its
name from the stripes marking the body, but
it is equally well-named for its ferociousness.

The raylike appearance of the angel shark of the family Squatinidae has little in common with the typical shark design Pictured here, the Pacific angel shark.

The angel shark is more reminiscent of the rays than any typical shark group. Like the ray, its pectoral fins are flat, its muscle and skeleton are dense and it swims by making vertical waves across its flattened fins.

The angel shark is a bottom-dweller, found in cool temperate waters along the continental shelves, where it feeds on small fish, squid, octopus, bivalves and sea snails.

The sandy color and pebble-like
markings of the angel shark serve
as camouflage. The angel will
lie half-buried in sand on the
ocean floor, ready to ambush
any small fish that swims near.

In the presence of as large an animal as man, an
angel shark is more likely to retreat than attack.
A rather sedentary predator, the angel shark will
sit motionless on the ocean bottom until a crustacean
or mollusc comes close enough to be "ambushed."

Photographing sharks is a tricky and often
dangerous business. Because shooting from a
distance and using a telephoto lens gives poor
results, the photographer must generally use
artificial light and get very close to the shark.
Many of the most striking photos of sharks were
taken by divers only five or six feet away.

A thresher shark (Alopias vulpinus) in mid-air. The thresher is a prize catch for the angler. Although it is often at the surface of the water, the approach of a fishing boat will send it to the bottom until it is safe again.

The thresher looks like any "average" shark until you get to the tail. The thresher's tail is often longer than the rest of its body and is used to surround its prey, schools of small fish. It may keep its food "corralled" with its tail for over an hour while it feeds.

The unmistakable long snout of the sawshark.
The "saw" is used as a weapon when attacking
its prey. Although decidedly fierce-looking, this
shark—a member of the small family
Pristiophoridae—is a shy bottom-dweller.

Pictured here, near Waroora in Western Australia, a tasselled
wobbegong. Belonging to the family Orectolobidae,
wobbegongs are bottom-dwellers with a relatively limited
distribution. Camouflaging lobes of skin at the sides of
the head are a distinguishing feature of the wobbegong.

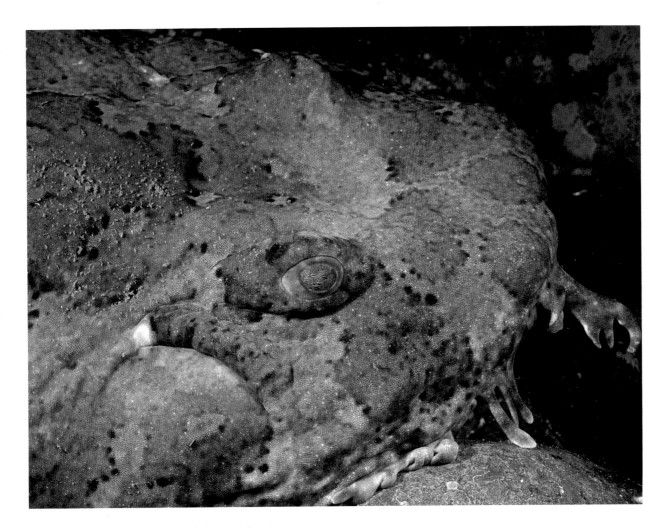

The broad head of the strangely marked, camouflaged
wobbegong, native to Australia and Papua New Guinea.

An extraordinary glimpse of
dochizame sharks reposing in a
cave of Japan's Izu Oceanic Park.
These "sleeping" sharks, like
those found in similar caves near
Mexico's Yucatan, prove that
sharks need not "swim or die"
as has often been believed.

This dochizame shark, in a "sleeping shark cave" in Japan,
appears to be dazed. Apparently, the natural conditions in such
caves cause the sharks to become tranquilized and sleepy.

Pictured here, a Hemiscyllium occillatum, or epaulette
shark, off the coast of Heron Island in Queensland. The
epaulette shark belongs to the family Hemiscylliidae
(or longtailed carpetsharks), and is distinguished by dark
patches at the sides of its head, which look like large eyes.

A carpet shark, with its large, dark
spots, moves sluggishly, and only as
far as necessary. The small caudal fin,
which acts as a modest paddle, does
not allow for much energetic swimming.

The dogfish sharks have perhaps the widest distribution of any shark family. Members of this group can be found from the Arctic to the Antarctic. Pictured here, the spiny dogfish, or Squalus acanthias.

Pictured here, the sevengill shark, a denizen of deep, cold waters. The sevengill has been known to attack spearfishing divers and steal their catch.

Similar in size to the whale shark, the basking shark (Cetorhinus maximus) can reach a length of 40 feet and more. It feeds on plankton, sailing into shoals of them with its mouth open for the feast. In an hour, the basking shark may swallow hundreds of pounds of this seafood, which individually are no larger than a thumbnail.

Profile of a deepwater shark caught in Japanese waters.
The shark is processed for use in a number of products,
from fish 'n' chips to squalene capsules made from
the shark's liver and said to benefit cancer victims.

A *deepwater shark, perhaps a crocodile shark*
(pseudocarcharius kamoharai) *which is notable
for its huge eyes and long, narrow-cusped teeth. Here, it is
hooked by a fishing line 500 meters below the surface.*

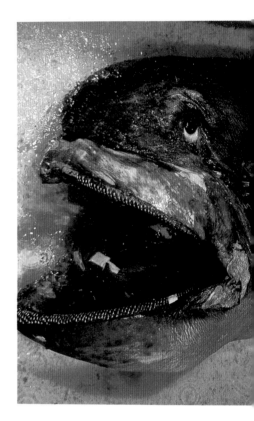

Megachasma pelagios, *or the*
megamouth shark, is a recent and
fascinating discovery. In a family
by itself—Megachasmidae—
the megamouth is one of only three
known filter-feeding sharks.
Only three megamouths have been
discovered since 1982.

Despite its angry visage and rows of hard, sharp teeth, the swellshark of the family Scyliorhinidae is no threat to humans. It averages less than four feet in length and prefers to dine on crustaceans and small or dead fish.

The swellshark is a slow-moving creature. It dwells on the ocean floor by day and is happy to collect its prey by merely holding its large mouth wide open, allowing fish to mistakenly swim inside.

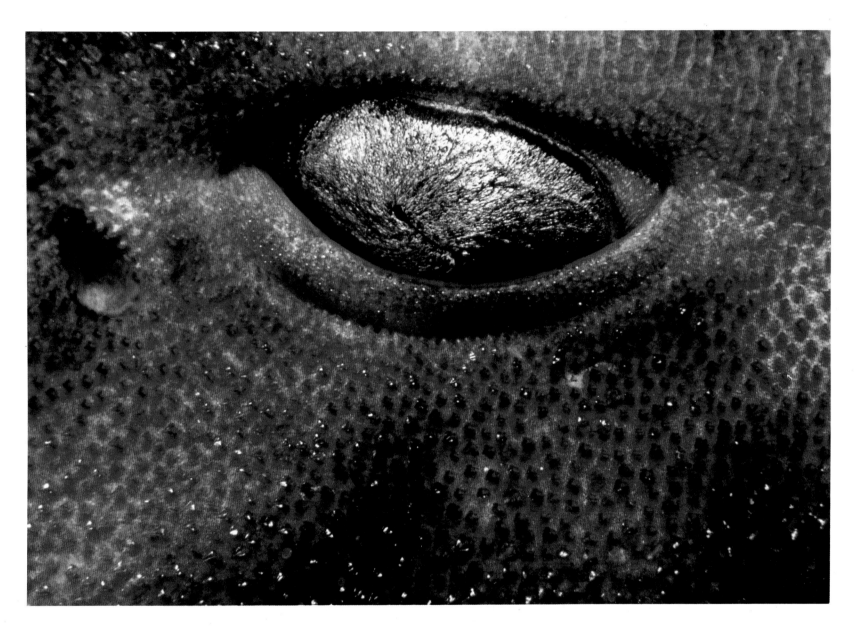

The eyes of the swellshark
(member of the family
Scyliorhinidae) are protected by a
thick fold of skin.

Here we have an extraordinary view of an egg case with yolk and hatchling swellshark visible within. After nearly a year, the egg case will split and the baby shark will emerge. On the back of the hatchling are two rows of oversized denticles which act as a ratchet, helping to force the shark out of the case. As soon as the swellshark leaves its case, it will begin to swim and hunt for crustaceans.

Here we see a very young swellshark. Once hatched, the baby swellshark is immediately able to swim and search out food.

The egg of the swellshark is laid in a green-gold egg case.
Amazingly, the cases come equipped with strings which attach
to strands of coral. An egg will take up to 10 months to hatch.

A horn shark swims by, on the lookout for dinner. Actually, the shark's eyes may be less crucial in hunting than its electroreceptors.

Here we see a baby horn shark. Horns are among the minority of egg-laying sharks. Two-thirds of all sharks are viviparous—born live.

Pictured, a horn shark with egg yolk. The horn
embryo is contained in its sac for a year. To protect them
from predators, the egg is covered by a capsule
which the mother deposits in hard-to-reach crevices.

The head of a swellshark. Its huge mouth will open so wide that fish will swim inside, not realizing they are about to be swallowed.

The swellshark gets its name from its ability to pump itself up with water or air. It is defensive behavior: a frightened swell shark will expand itself in a rock crevice, or some other narrow hiding place, making it immovable.

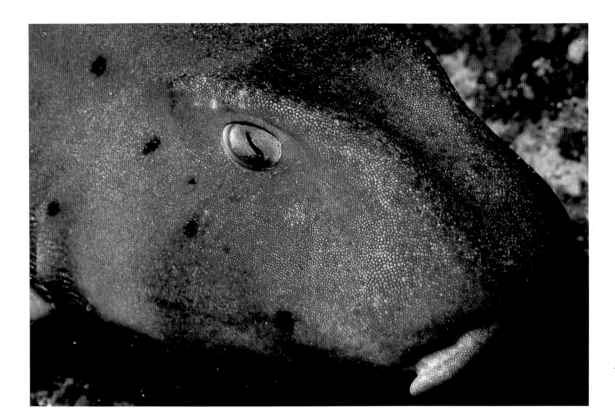

The horn shark moves very little, preferring to sit and wait for its prey. For this reason their distribution is relatively restricted.

The horn shark will hide in caves, gullies and under beds of kelp, waiting to spring on its prey of smaller creatures.

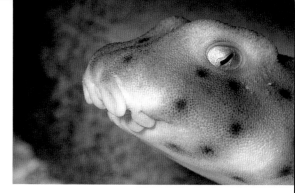

A horn shark, posing for a close-up. The horn is widely known as the "pig shark." However, its family name—Heterodontus—means "different teeth," referring to the cobbled crushing and cutting teeth peculiar to this group.

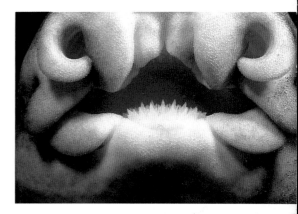

Known as the "pig shark" because of its distinctive snout, the teeth of the horn shark are also distinctive, made up of cutters and crushers, for breaking up its favored menu of shellfish.

The horn gets its name from the spines on the dorsal fins. Its pectoral fins are unusually strong, allowing it to climb rocks in pursuit of sea urchins and other prey.

A horn shark will often limit its domain to a single
archipelago or small area of the sea. It is a nocturnal feeder,
preying on sea urchins, crustaceans and other small molluscs.

A horn shark, resting on the ocean floor, where it may spend
the entire day. A member of the family Heterodontidae,
the horn shark prefers temperate and tropical waters.

A leopard shark, or Triakis semifasciata, *with its distinctive spotted markings. Leopard sharks, along with few other species, are remarkable in that they have shown the greatest longevity in captivity.*

Camouflaged by its markings, the leopard shark can rest safely on the ocean floor. A member of the family Triakidae (or, more commonly, "houndsharks"), it is a shy bottom-dweller, for whom attack without provocation is unknown.

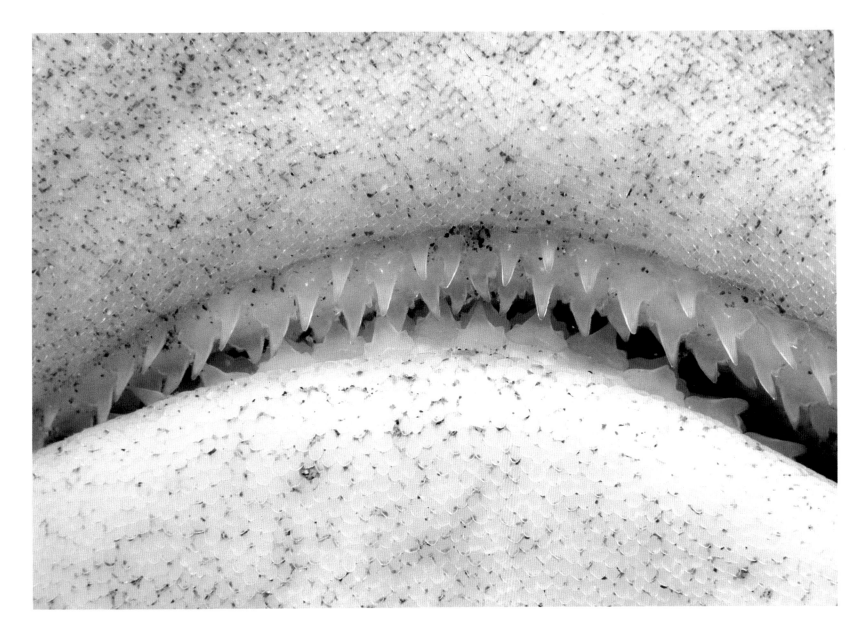

The shape of a shark's teeth varies
from species to species. They are
modified according to their typical
prey—long and narrow for
grasping fish, small and sharp
for crushing crustaceans.

The lemon shark (Negaprion
brevirostris) is slow to grow, taking
up to 15 years to mature and
reproduce. The lemon shark's ability
to replace itself is very limited as
pregnancy takes close to a year and
only occurs every two years.
Overfishing of the lemon shark could
easily put the species in jeopardy.

The lemon shark gets its name from the yello
coloring on its sides and back. It is foun
primarily in the warmer waters of the Atlant
seaboard. Frequenting shallo
inshore waters, the lemon shark has occasional
attacked bathers in Florida and the Bahama

A sand tiger shark enters a cave, 30 feet below the surface in the Bonin Islands, Japan. Sand tigers, members of the family Odontaspididae often swim with their mouths open, exposing long, sharp teeth.

Pictured here, a bull or Zambezi shark, often found deep within fresh water lakes and rivers. A member of the family Carcharhinididae, it is a requiem shark, known for its ferocity.

Here we see the large pores leading up to and along the shark's snout which are connected to the ampullae of Lorenzini. The ampullae help the shark detect objects in the water by means of electroreception.

The tiger shark (Galeocerdo cuvier) is one of the most feared creatures on land or sea. It is a confirmed man-eater, and swimmers would be well-advised to avoid nightbathing, as night is the time the tiger shark is most likely to hunt in shallow water.

Tiger sharks are large and dangerous predators. They have been reported at lengths in excess of 17 feet and often cruise well-touristed beaches for food.

Sand tigers, members of the family Odontaspididae,
enter a cave below the water's surface in the Bonin Islands, Japan.

A fisherman sees the grim outline of a tiger shark. The tiger is found off the southern coasts of the United States and will feed in very shallow water. This makes it a great threat to swimmers.

Pictured, baby tiger sharks. Unlike other requiem sharks of the family Carcharhinididae, tiger sharks are ovoviviparous—produced from eggs hatched within the female's body.

Pictured here is the sand tiger shark, with its mouth agape. A sand tiger's teeth, although giving the shark a particularly dangerous appearance, are adapted to catching and holding prey that is often small enough to be swallowed whole.

The nurse shark, a member of the family Ginglymostomatidae, is most easily identified by the twin barbels on the snout. Although they have the appearance of long fangs, they are fleshy features and are there to provide the shark with a sense of touch.

The nurse shark is a relatively lazy creature, spending much of its time resting on the ocean floor. It is a nocturnal feeder, whose prey consists of snails, lobster, crabs and sea urchins.

The grey nurse shark is a relatively nonaggressive shark. Belonging as it does to the family Odontaspididae, it is distinguished by its ragged toothed appearance. The grey nurse prefers such prey as bony fishes, large crustaceans and small sharks.

Eugomphodus taurus, or the grey nurse
shark, often swims with its mouth open.
Because of its rather ferocious appearance,
the grey nurse has been hunted almost
to the point of extinction. It is now a
protected species in Australia.

A remora with its host, a nurse shark. The nurse shark
will sit on the sea floor to be serviced by cleaner fish who
remove various parasites. While being cleaned, the nurse
may stop all gill movement for as long as two minutes.

"Feeding frenzies" are often associated with the grey reef shark, or Carcharhinus amblyrhynchos. In a feeding frenzy, the sharks will become completely unaware of their surroundings as they lash out, biting anything in their way.

The grey reef shark will react to a div. harassing or following it with its distincti. threat display. The shark may turn i. figure eights of small circles, the hea. swaying from side to side. In the final sta. of the display, the shark hunches its bac. lowers its pectoral fins, and holds its mou. open. Frozen in this position, the shark w. begin to sink for a moment before snappin. into terrifying action, attacking t. perceived antagonist with a deadly bi.

Pictured, two short-nosed grey reef sharks in the Red
Sea, near Sinai. A blunter nose, as well as a white
marking on the edge of its dorsal fin, differentiates
this grey reef shark from its Pacific cousin.

The male's aggressive courting techniques leave this female grey reef shark (Carcharhinus amblyrhynchos) with noticeable bite marks. Evolution has provided the female with a tougher skin than the male, in order to help them survive the rigors of this mating.

A group of mating grey reef sharks, at Ras Muhammed in the Red Sea. The grey reef sharks, like most requiems, are viviparous, giving birth after a gestation period of up to a year.

Male and female grey reef sharks perform a vicious courtship dance. When the female has swum off alone, her prospective mate approaches and bites the female about the body and fins, often leaving severe gouges.

The grey reef shark, or Carcharhinus
amblyrhynchos, is the major predator along the
coral reefs of the Indo-Pacific and the Red Sea.
Like many of the sharks responsible for attacks on
humans, the grey reef is a requiem—a term
connoting danger—of the family Carcharhinididae.

A remora, sometimes known as a sucker fi
hitches a ride with a short-nosed grey reef sha
The remora can attach itself to a shark by mea
of a dorsal fin, which acts like a suction dev

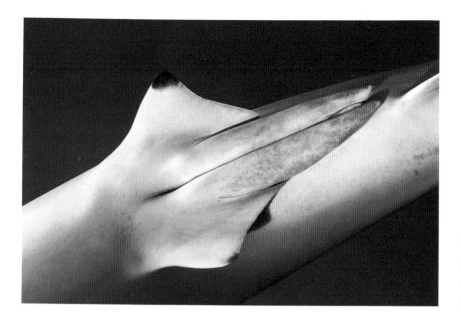

The male shark fertilizes the female by means of intromittent organs called claspers, located below the pelvic fins. The male shark inserts the claspers in the female shark's reproductive opening, the cloaca.

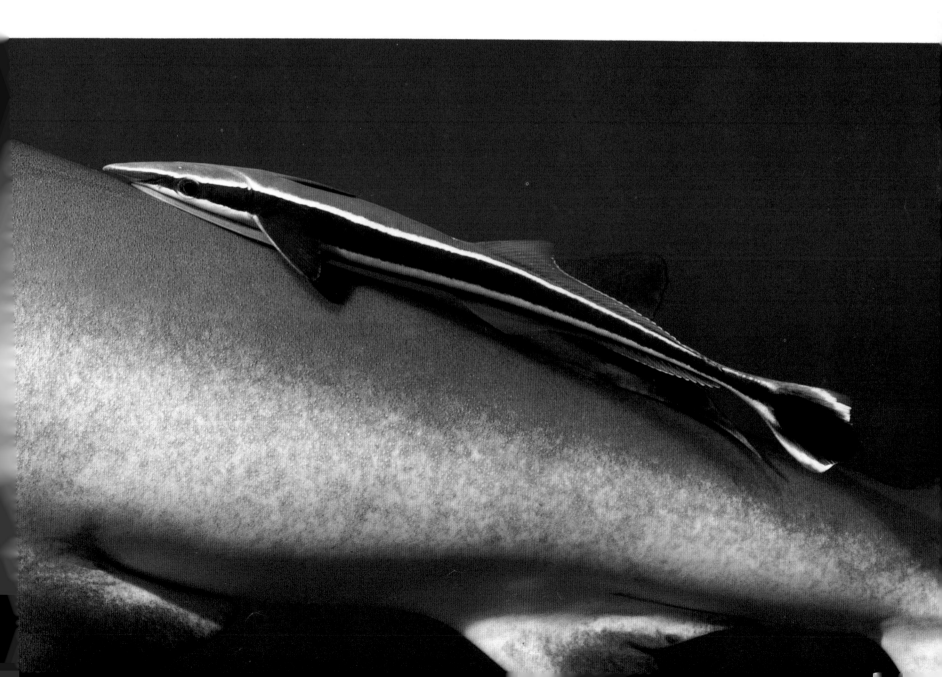

A whitetip reef shark
(Triaenodon obesus) in a
cave. The whitetip reef sharks will
comb the reef looking for fish
resting in holes in the coral.
The sharks themselves enjoy
resting in the crevices of the
coral, often stacking themselves
three or four sharks high.

The typical size for the whitetip
reef shark is five feet. It is a shy
and unaggressive creature,
keeping close to the sea floor and
hiding in crevices in the coral reef.
The whitetip reef feeds on small
fish, octopuses, lobsters and crabs.

An intelligent and peaceful fish, the whitetip reef shark can be trained to take food from a diver's hand. On reefs where there is a good deal of spearfishing, these whitetips have been known to follow a diver and wait for a handout.

In the immense depths of the
Pacific, an oceanic whitetip shark.
The oceanic whitetip is distributed
widely throughout the tropical
waters of the world.

The oceanic whitetip shark (Carcharhinus
longimanus) is recognizable from the white
markings on the dorsal and pectoral fins.
In pursuit of prey, including tuna, dolphin and
marlin, it is capable of moving at incredible speeds.

The oceanic whitetip shark, or Carcharhinus
longimanus, *at home in deep, tropical waters.*
This shark, a member of the family Carcharhinididae,
prefers a depth of anywhere from 60 to 1,500 meters.

The oceanic whitetip shark is found worldwide in
tropical and sub-tropical waters. It is found almost exclusively
in deep water, but will come close to shore around the
Hawaiian islands. This photo was taken off the Kona Coast.

The blacktip shark lives on a diet of fish and has a particular fondness for stingrays. It is quite similar to the spinner shark except for its slimmer body, smaller eyes and more extended snout. It is not considered dangerous to humans.

Carcharhinus limbatus, or the blacktip shark, is a requiem shark of the family Carcharhinididae. Less is known about this species than others that are found in the same habitat, and perhaps for this reason it is considered potentially dangerous.

A blacktip shark cruising just above the ocean floor. There are 350 species of shark, ranging in size from 12 inches to the 60 feet and more of the whale shark. The blacktip, at six to eight feet, is an average-sized shark.

Individual blue sharks (Prionace glauca) can travel incredible distances. In a study of tagged blues, scientists found that these sharks traveled from England to as far away as Brazil.

The blue shark is a requiem shark of the family Carcharhinididae. It is the family responsible for most of the attacks on humans, yet some divers consider the blue a relative "pussy cat." It can be easily fended off with a hit or shove. Yet the blue shark can become excited and aggressive, and the presence of blood in the water will cause the blue shark to attack.

Pictured here is a male blue shark off the coast of
California. In summer, the blues may practice sexual
segregation. Males will be found in warmer temperate waters
while the females confine themselves to the colder north.

The blue shark travels widely. It is found in cool and warm ocean waters throughout the world. In the tropics it will stay in the cooler deep waters, but in temperate areas it will swim closer to the surface.

With its long pectoral fins, the blue shark is able to swim at a slow pace and not sink. It is, however, also capable of sudden bursts of speed.

Squid are a favorite food of the blue shark. When a blue shark comes upon a concentration of squid it will charge back and forth through them, mouth wide open, swallowing as many as he can. When the shark cannot fit any more squid into its body, it will vomit in order to make room for more.

99

The hammerhead is an extremely
maneuverable creature. The shape
of its head may aid this, acting
as a forward planing surface.

The scalloped hammerhead shark
(Sphyrna lewini). The head of
the hammerhead is five times
as wide as it is long and quite
flat. Sensory organs of the snout
are dispersed along the whole
of the "hammer."

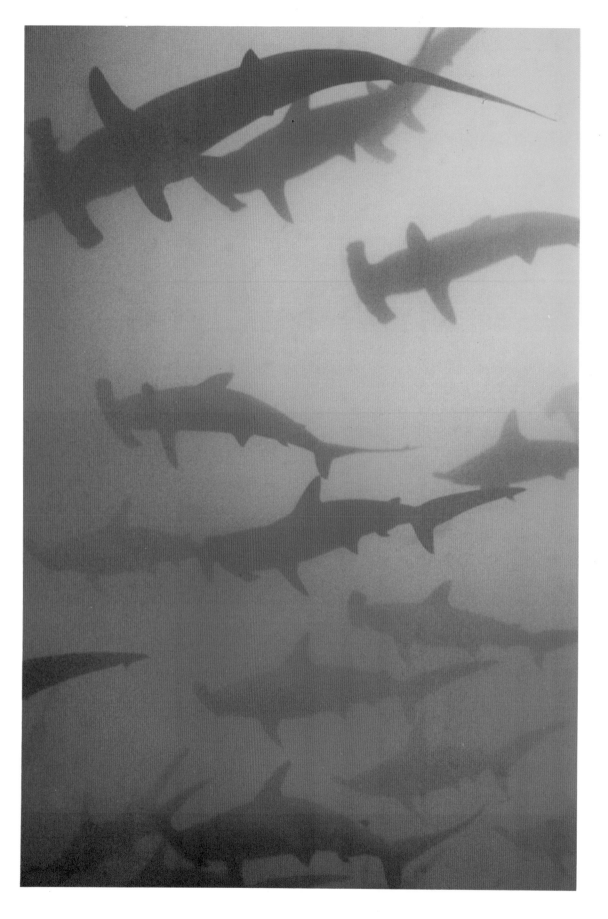

A large group of scalloped hammerheads, or Sphyrna lewini. The photographer had to free dive below 25 meters to shoot this gathering—the noise of scuba bubbles will scare them away.

Hammerhead sharks are found in all warm temperate and tropical seas. They confine themselves to coastal and inshore waters, so the sighting of one would not be surprising.

Despite its size and the power of its jaws, the hammerhead has a reputation for shyness around humans. Still, they will attack a diver and have been known to steal a speared fish from a diver.

In the Coral Sea, underwater explorer and shark expert Ron Taylor
approaches a great hammerhead, or Sphyrna mokkaran. It is the largest
of the hammerheads, as well as the most powerful and aggressive.

A 45-foot whale shark (Rhiniodon typus) *is by no means unusual,*
and there have been confirmed sightings of 60-footers.
Marine biologists believe they may come even larger.

For all its length and broad body, the whale shark moves with effortless grace, powered along by its huge tail. The gentle whale shark will obligingly give divers a free ride on its back, as in this photo, but an accidental collision with the powerful tail can cause serious injury.

The unique and beautiful spotted pattern of the whale shark. The spots range in size from that of a grape to that of a grapefruit.

Near the Maldives Island, a whale sha (Rhiniodon typus), its broad mou open for feeding. The whale shark fee primarily on plankton, but will sometim rise up through a school of tuna or oth fish, swallowing them as it surface

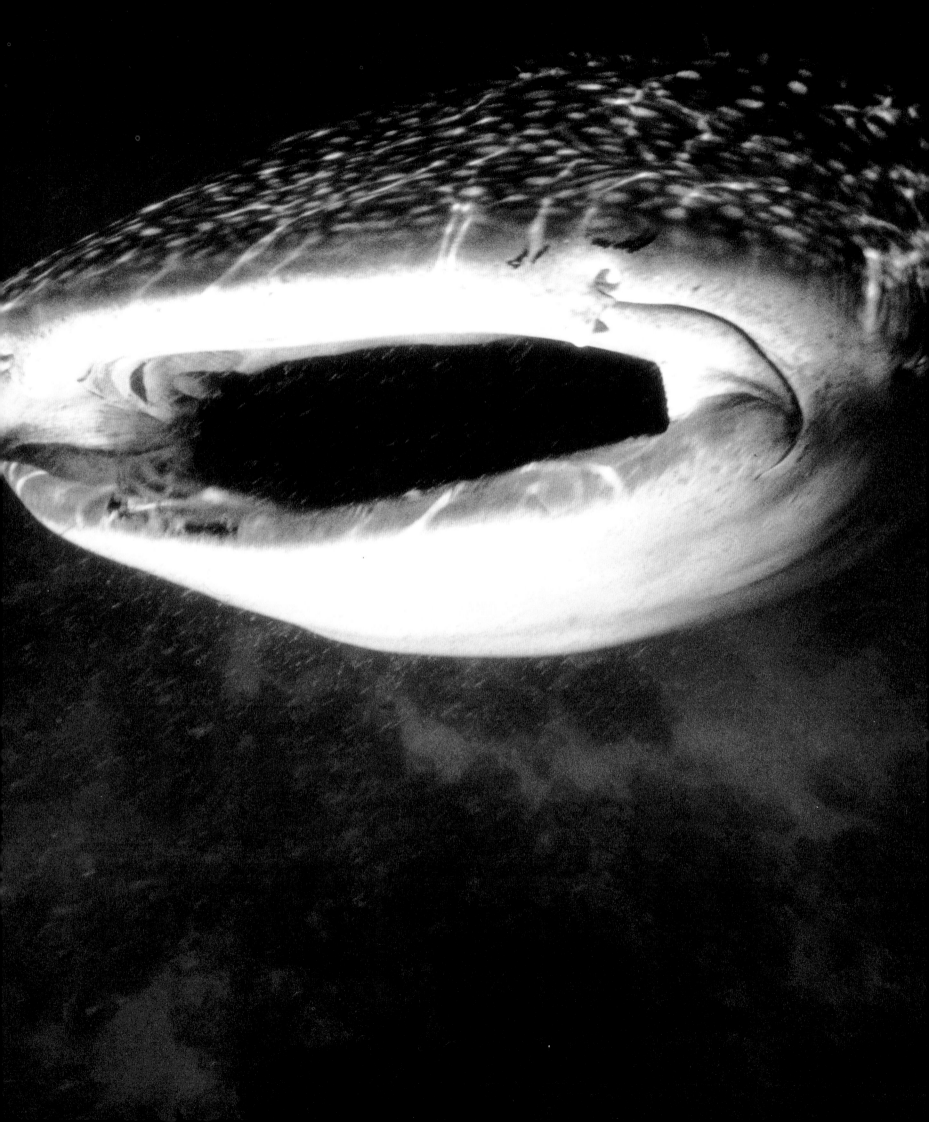

The predatory white shark. Forever on a hunt for prey, the great white will devour turtles, seals, sea lions, other sharks and humans. Great whites as small as 10 feet have been captured and cut open to reveal whole sea lions and, once, a six-foot-tall man. Imagine, then, the appetite of a 40-foot specimen.

The great white shark (Carcharodon carcharias) is not a picky eater. Like other large predators it must be flexible in its diet in order to find enough food to live on.

The teeth of the great white shark are undoubtedly its most terrifying feature. They are long, triangular, sharp and steel-strong daggers, perfectly designed for tearing off chunks of flesh from the shark's large prey.

For all the media attention and legend attached to the great white shark as a man-eater, there have been relatively few attacks proven to be the work of the great white. Off the coast of California, where these sharks are common, there have been only four fatalities in the last 30 years.

A great white approaches a diver in a shark-proof cage.
Not even the high-tensile steel of the cage is a guarantee
that it will withstand the attack of an angered great white.

A shark cage is the perfect place to get a close photograph of an agitated great white. The cages are made to hold up to extreme levels of force, but even so, there are cases of great whites ripping them open.

A great white shark takes the bait outside a shark cage. A diver stands within the cage taking photos. Shark cages have gaps to allow more room for the photographer to maneuver his camera, and these have occasionally allowed an angry shark inside the cage.

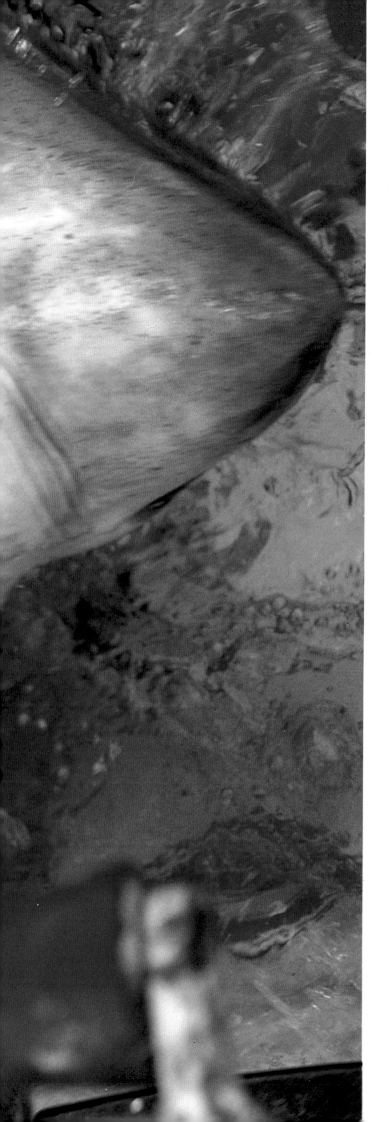

For many, a fearful emblem of the shark: the streamlined
fin of a great white at the water's surface. While they have
a reputation as man-eaters out of proportion to their actual
rate of attack, the great white will attack and consume
humans, possibly mistaking them for seals or sea lions.

A great white shark (Carcharodon carcharias)
attacks a bait of horsemeat with speed and fury. The great
white is easily lured by a bloody bait, able to leap above
the water and rush at the bait, ripping through it with
frightening ferocity.

The great white shark is a magnificent—if sometimes deadly—creature.
It is a creature of great intelligence, with excellent visual acuity, hearing and smell.

*The streamlined, torpedo-like shape of the great white
shark was designed by nature around 30 million years ago.*

Among many species, a larger shark will feed on a smaller one. Because of this, survival of some species depends on segregation by size.

Pictured, a great white shark—16 feet-long, weighing approximately 3,000 pounds— attacks a diver in a small abalone cage.

Pictured, a great white shark rising six feet out of the water to tear into some bloody bait. Attracting a great white to your boat is a risky business; a frustrated or annoyed great white has been known to damage or destroy seacraft.

The photographer encounters a great white shark.
The white shark is on an almost constant quest for food.
While it has been known to devour humans, its preferred
diet includes seals, sea lions and other sharks.

Although it is found in tropic waters, the great white shark has a preference
for a colder water temperature, such as the central coast of California. Many attacks on
humans in the tropics are incorrectly attributed to the great white merely because of
its notoriety as a man-killer and without any concern for its natural habitat.

Sharks of one type or another are present in
nearly every marine environment, from warm tropic
to icy arctic waters, from shallow reefs and rocky
coastlines to the vast depths of mid-ocean.

Pictured here, a close-up of the eye of a blue shark,
or Prionace glauca. In evidence is the tapetum,
the mirror-like plates on the retina of the eye which
aid the vision of the shark. As an active pelagic
predator, the blue shark typically has larger eyes
than those of bottom-dwelling sharks.

n angry-looking great white (Carcharodon
rcharias) bursts through the ocean surface. Its
th are rows of razor-like spikes. The great white
master of its domain, a superpredator.

The wobbegong shark is found in the Western Pacific, primarily off the coasts of Australia and New Guinea. Their unusual, often indescribable markings—splotches, dots and stripes—provide camouflage against rocky or sandy sea bottom.

A swellshark shows off its rows of razor-sharp teeth. As the teeth in front wear out, teeth in the next row move forward into place. This process of replacing the teeth continues for the shark's whole life.

A blue shark (Prionace glauca) feasts a mackerel. The insides of the blue shar gills form a fine mesh through which sm crustaceans—such as shrimps and crabs cannot escape, as well as trapping larger pr

Pictured here, a mako shark.
The mako will grow to 12 feet
in length and may weigh as
much as a thousand pounds.
Makos travel the globe, but are
often found in great numbers
off the coast of New England.

Grey reef sharks (Carcharhinus amblyrhynchos)
will hover at points on the reef where the currents are strongest
and where they are most likely to find a potential meal.

The oceanic whitetip shark
(Carcharhinus longimanus)—
Jacques Cousteau called it the most
dangerous of all sharks. When
investigating a potential prey it is
fearless and lethal, willing to
attack anything without hesitation.
Its triangular, serrated teeth can
rip huge chunks from its prey.

blue shark, or Prionace
lauca, with its long, pointed
ead and snout. Although blue
arks can be relatively
onaggressive, they are members
the family Carcharhinididae, to
hich most sharks who are
sponsible for attacks belong.

Index by Photographer

Index by Page

•Identifications, where necessary, appear in the Index by Photographer in front of the page number.